PATTY NUN

# IN SPITE
# OF IT ALL

## AN ACCOUNT OF ADULTERY, RAPE AND MURDER

**CLAY BRIDGES**
P R E S S

**In Spite of it All**
A Story About Adultery, Rape, and Murder

Copyright © 2021 by Patty Nun

Published by Clay Bridges in Houston, TX
www.ClayBridgesPress.com

All rights reserved. No part of this publication may be reproduced, stored in a retrieval system, or transmitted in any form by any means, electronic, mechanical, photocopy, recording, or otherwise, without the prior permission of the publisher, except as provided for by USA copyright law.

ISBN: 978-1-68488-001-0
eISBN: 978-1-68488-000-3

*Dedicated*
*To*
# *Bathsheba*

- *Widow of Uriah the Hittite*
- *Wife of King David*
- *Mother of Solomon, Nathan, Shobab, and Shammua*
- *Queen Mother*
- *Ruler of Israel with King Solomon*

# Table of Contents

| | |
|---|---:|
| Chapter One | 1 |
| Chapter Two | 13 |
| Chapter Three | 29 |
| Chapter Four | 37 |
| Chapter Five | 43 |
| Chapter Six | 59 |
| Acknowledgments | 69 |

# CHAPTER ONE

The evening was eerie quiet; yet, peaceful in the city of Jerusalem. With all the Israeli troops at war, the streets were nearly empty. Here and there a few old men dotted the streets. Most were men too old to go to battle. It was dusk and children were in their homes with their mothers and grandmothers preparing their evening meal. The seven wives, ten concubines, and numerous children that lived in the king's palace were in their various quarters, each also preparing for the evening's meal followed by the bedtime routine for the children. King David's multiple servants, bodyguards, chefs, cupbearers, gardeners, councilmen, advisors, messengers, royal scribes, and more, were available twenty-four hours a day to meet the king's every need.

In the tenth century BC, war was a way of life. Fifty-year-old King David, the second king of the United Kingdom of Israel and Judah, administered justice and righteousness for all his people. He had captured the Canaanite Jebusite fortress stronghold city of Zion and made it his home. He called

## In Spite of it All

it the city of David. It became known as Jerusalem, and he established it as the nation's capital. Joab, his nephew, was commander over the army; Jehoshaphat kept the records; Zadok and Abimelech were priests; Shavsha was the secretary; Benaiah, was commander over several armies; and King David's sons were the chief officials who served at his side. He had developed a strong military defense and was undefeated on the battlefield. The kingdom of Israel had reached 60,000 square miles. David had demonstrated twenty years of astonishing and admired leadership, and his popularity was at an all-time high. David became greater and greater, for the Lord God of hosts was with him.

Hiram, king of Tyre, sent messengers to David with cedar trees and carpenters and stonemasons; and they built a house for David. The timbers were hauled from Tyre to the Phoenician coast and then sailed by the Mediterranean Sea to the port of Jaffa. The timbers were then carried overland by cart the thirty miles to Jerusalem.

David had prepared, in Jerusalem, a central place of worship for all Israel, a pitched tent or tabernacle, where the Ark of the Covenant was to reside. He and all the house of Israel brought the Ark of God up from the house of Obed-Edom the Gittite, to the city of David with gladness. There was a procession, music, offerings, dance, sacrifices, and distribution of food. King David danced wearing the linen ephod, a

## Chapter One

priestly garment. This was the Ark of the Covenant, which God commanded Moses to make more than four hundred years ago! It was a wood box, but completely covered with gold and had an ornate gold top known as the mercy seat. David appointed Asaph to direct ministers before the Ark of the Lord, to invoke, to thank, and to praise the God of Israel. David then started making plans for the Temple of the Lord to permanently reside in a building in Jerusalem. He had money, power, authority, and fame. Everything he touched seemed to turn to gold. The Lord was with him and had given him success.

It was the main task of kings to lead their armies to battle after the spring rains. However, one particular spring after the rains had subsided, King David chose to stay home. He sent his top commanding officer Joab, his servants, and the whole army of Israel to destroy the sons of Ammon and besiege the city of Rabbah, the capital city of the Ammonites. While his soldiers were camping in an open field, David was indulging himself in his palace pleasures. Things were becoming pretty easy for David. He seemed to have forgotten his success was the result of God blessing his efforts.

He had leisure time on his hands since he had been staying home from war, and had grown a bit bored and melancholy. He had been taking afternoon naps lately. Something to do to fill up his afternoon, as his days were long. He had just

## In Spite of it All

gotten up from a late afternoon nap and was sitting on the edge of his bed. He considered sending for one of his wives or concubines to come to his chambers for his pleasure and satisfaction. He couldn't remember, though, who was next in line, which was pregnant with his next child, who was caring for sick and/or unruly children, or who was at a time in her show of blood that sexual relations was forbidden by the Law of Moses. And besides, they were all busy with the evening meal and activities.

It was impossible to keep up with his family's emotional needs. He generously provided for the physical needs of his wives, concubines, children, and servants. They had palace security, clothing, and the finest food available. His children had the best Jewish instructors the kingdom had to offer, who came to the palace and instructed his sons in Jewish history and the Law of Moses. David was proud of his sons when he heard them recite from memory the Five Books of Moses.

He stood up from his seated position on the edge of the bed, pulled on his robe, slipped his feet into his sandals, and ran his fingers through his graying hair. He stroked his beard as he walked out of his bedroom chambers onto the patio roof of his palace. He was restless.

King David's bedchamber was on the second floor of the palace and had a door that opened onto a patio roof. Both the

## Chapter One

king's bedroom and patio roof were elegantly and lavishly furnished. He would use the patio roof to sit with his family or with his men in counsel. It was situated above the public demands and away from the streets, and situated in such a place as people from the street or nearby houses could not spot him. The palace windows were screened by latticework. David's palace was built on the highest point of the city of Jerusalem. Thus, he had a view of the houses stretching down the slopes surrounding the palace.

David walked around on his rooftop patio. He stopped because his attention was drawn to a very beautiful woman who was bathing in the courtyard of her home. Since it was dusk, he had to strain to see what he did see. His heart raced, as he knew he was viewing forbidden territory. His feet seemed stuck to the patio floor, as his eyes stayed fixed on the woman. He liked what he saw and enjoyed the moment. He watched her stand up and step out of the water. Her maidservant wrapped a towel around the woman and she walked into the house.

For a few minutes, David considered the beautiful woman he had seen and how to deal with his emotional response. He fantasized how it would feel to kiss her as he took her in his arms. His lust for her became overwhelming. He paced back and forth on his patio for several minutes. Pondering. Contemplating. Finally, he called for his messenger. David said,

## In Spite of it All

"Who is the woman that lives in the house down there?" as he pointed with his hand in the direction he saw her bathing. And one said, "Is this not Bathsheba, the daughter of Eliam, the wife of Uriah the Hittite?"

---

*He recalled Eliam and Uriah were both on the battlefield fighting on his behalf with the army of Israel against the Amalekites. He had sent them off. They were spot-on soldiers. Uriah had been a high official in the Hittite army and an inhabitant of the Jebusite city, Jerusalem, which was the home of many Hittites, when David and his army conquered Jerusalem and made it the new capital of Israel. The Israelites lived among the Canaanites, Hittites, Amorites, Perizzites, Hivites, and Jebusites. After David conquered the Jebusite city, the Hittites and Jebusites were assimilated into the Israelite culture and later some embraced the Jewish faith.*

*It was at this time Uriah renounced the pagan gods of his fathers, converted to Judaism, and changed his name to Uriah. Uriah meant "The Flame of God." The first part of his conversion ceremony included submission to brit milah. Circumcision is an outward physical sign of the covenant between God and Abraham and his descendants. The rabbi recited a blessing over Uriah before his circumcision covenant.*

## Chapter One

*"Blessed are You, Lord our God, King of the universe, Who has sanctified us with His commandments and commanded us concerning circumcision."*

*Seven days later Uriah completed his conversion ceremony by a ritual, full immersion in a mikveh. A mikveh is a ritual purification bath all Jews observe. He had now entered into the covenant of Israel and was one of God's chosen people. It was a privilege worshipping the One and true God of Abraham, Isaac, and Jacob, not because he had to, but because he wanted to. As a proselyte Jew, he enjoyed all the privileges and responsibilities as a full member of the Jewish population. He could now participate in Jewish holidays and ceremonies and worship at the Tent of Meeting.*

*Even while fighting with the Hittite army, Uriah had admired David from afar and recognized his military strategy was the best in the land. After his Jebusite city had been defeated by the Israeli army, and the dust settled, he sent word to David he had converted to Judaism, and it would be a privilege to serve in his army - if he would have him.*

*David accepted Uriah's offer to serve and he did so with such bravery and skill that he was invited to become a part of David's Thirty Mighty Men who served as his personal bodyguards and as key commanders in his army. These were men known for heroic feats. As a member of this elite unit, Uriah*

## In Spite of it All

*fought alongside others like Eliam, the son of one of David's advisors.*

*Eliam and Uriah served together in the Israeli army for several years and added to their accomplishments as brave warriors. They worked together both on and off the battlefield. As part of this elite unit of King David's soldiers, Uriah took his position seriously and was a loyal and obedient servant to the king. Eliam was impressed with the professionalism and dedication Uriah brought to the Israeli army. He was satisfied he had converted to Judaism, not just because of peer pressure, but because he saw the need in his life to serving the One true God. Eliam's father, Ahithophel, was David's closest advisor. He was filled with wisdom as if one inquired from the Word of God. All three, along with David's top advisors and soldiers, were frequent guests of the palace.*

*When Eliam's daughter Bathsheba turned thirteen years of age, he made arrangements with Uriah for a betrothal ceremony between them. As was the custom of the day, the fathers arranged the match, and the prospective bride was consulted by her father and asked if she wanted to marry the man. However, in this situation, since Uriah had left his pagan gods and his family had disowned him, Eliam approached Uriah about marrying his daughter. Eliam asked Bathsheba if she wanted to marry Uriah and she agreed to the engagement.*

## Chapter One

*Both Uriah and Eliam met at Uriah's quarters and negotiated a bride price for Bathsheba. As she was both a virgin and very beautiful in appearance, her bride price was set high, at fifty shekels, in the event they would divorce or Uriah would be killed in battle. Both Eliam and Uriah signed in triplicate the ketubah or marriage contract, with one copy given to Eliam, one copy given to Uriah, and one copy filed at the Tent of Meeting. It was a legally binding contract between the two families. After the contract was signed, Uriah and Bathsheba were legally married. However, the marriage was not consummated, nor did the couple live together. Bathsheba continued to live in her parent's home, and Uriah, age thirty-one, had quarters provided him near the palace as an officer of King David's Israeli army.*

*Their engagement of twelve months was a time of separation where both the bride and groom each prepared emotionally and spiritually for the wedding day. According to Jewish Law of Warfare, a man betrothed to a woman, even though not married, was exempt from military service, lest he died in the battle and another man marry her. Uriah prepared his home for Bathsheba and Bathsheba, her mother and grandmother, prepared her wedding clothes.*

*At the end of the twelve months of preparations, Bathsheba and her virgin companions waited anxiously for Uriah and his male companions to come to Eliam's house to fetch her.*

## In Spite of it All

*Bathsheba had taken the mikveh ritual purification bath with the assistance of her female companions. They braided her hair with borrowed precious stones and she was adorned like a queen. Her wedding attire was complete with a veil on her head.*

*As anticipated, Uriah dressed like a king, and his companions made their way to Eliam's house late in the afternoon. Uriah actually had tears in his eyes when he saw his very beautiful bride, Bathsheba, as she stood waiting for him in the house. He took her hand and together they led the procession from Eliam's house through the streets of Jerusalem. The street was lit with oil lamps held by the guests. Uriah and Bathsheba heard singing and music along the way. She felt like a queen and it seemed to her she floated down the street in the arms of her groom as they proceeded to Uriah's quarters.*

*At Uriah's quarters, he carried Bathsheba over the threshold into the room he had prepared for their consummation. The wedding guests waited outside. The bloodstained bed-coverings were evident to selected guests that fourteen-year-old Bathsheba was a virgin. The wedding feast lasted seven days. There was plenty of food, dancing, and drinking. King David attended one of the days of the wedding celebration.*

## Chapter One

"Is there anything else, King David?" asked the messenger. David hesitated only for a moment as guilt crept into his thoughts, but he logically and quickly reasoned them away and said, "Yes. Wait until the stars are out before leaving the palace. Then take another messenger with you and take Bathsheba from her home, and bring her back to the palace. Enter through the servant's lower side entrance." As soldiers to the king, they took an oath of obedience and confidence. Thus, all activities and guests within the king's chambers were kept secret.

While waiting for Bathsheba, David changed into a comfortable robe, one he only wore when inviting his wives to his quarters. He ordered two evening meals from the kitchen, had a flask of his best wine sent up from the wine cellar, buffed two golden goblets, checked the wicks in the oil lamps, tidied up his chambers, and fluffed pillows. As the king, he had never tidied up his chambers before and was a bit awkward picking up after himself. That was left for his maidservants. However, this evening he wanted the room to look extraordinary as he walked around making slight adjustments here and there with the decor. He could feel the cool evening breeze blowing into his bedroom chambers through the open door to his patio. He walked out onto

## In Spite of it All

the patio and stood looking in the direction of Bathsheba's house. It was dark now and he could not see her house. The stars were just making themselves known in the night sky.

He heard a knock on his door. As king of Israel, he had twenty-four-hour security, seven days a week. He was never without protection, and always had the authority to call security soldiers if he felt threatened or heard rumors he was going to be overthrown. He was quite aware two security soldiers were standing immediately outside his bedroom chambers every minute.

David walked to the door and through the closed door asked, "Who is it?" "Your soldiers, King David," replied one of the soldiers. David opened the door. Bathsheba stood between the two soldiers. He could see his security guards on either side of the door to his chambers. "King David, I present you Lady Bathsheba," said one of the messengers. "That is all," said David. "I do not want to be disturbed." The messengers bowed to the king as they left Bathsheba standing alone in the doorway. David took her hand, led her over the threshold, and closed the door to his chambers behind him.

He lay with her as he engaged in an adulterous one-night affair.

# CHAPTER TWO

David, a descendant of Miriam, the sister of Moses, was born in Bethlehem in 1040 BC and was the youngest of eight sons of Jesse and Nitzevet. Jesse was a noble and respected poor Jewish shepherd and an ancestor of the Jewish Tribe of Judah. David's great grandfather, Boaz, was the judge of Bethlehem, and his grandfather, Obed, was in service to the Lord.

David first learned about the God of Abraham, Isaac and Jacob, and the law, from Jesse, when he was only three years old. His religious and formal education started at five years of age at the House of the Book where he listened to his Jewish instructors read from the five Books of Moses. His instructors emphasized the importance of memorization. At age thirteen he was responsible for observing the commandments, evident by his public Bar Mitzvah ceremony marking his rite into manhood. At thirteen he also lead worship services in the Tent of the Meeting, read from the Torah, and gave sermons.

## In Spite of it All

As the youngest son, he was to look after his father's flocks in the fields. He was handsome in appearance, with bright eyes and skin having a fresh and healthy red color. David remembers the day he was called from his father's fields. He was only fifteen years old. One of his father's servants came to the field where David was tending sheep and said, "You are to go home. They want you back at the house."

As Prophet Samuel came into Bethlehem that day, the elders sitting at the city gate came trembling to meet him and said, "Do you come in peace?" It was still on their minds how recently Samuel hewed to pieces King Agag of the Amalekites at Gilgal who was enemies of Israel. Samuel said, "In peace, I have come to sacrifice a heifer to the Lord. Consecrate yourselves and come with me to the sacrifice." He also consecrated Jesse and his sons and invited them to the sacrifice. Consecration included prayer, liturgical washing to cleanse themselves, and sacrifice of a lamb.

Samuel did not express the nature of his business in town. Tucked deep inside his heart he had heard God tell him that from the house of Jesse in the city of Bethlehem, the next king of Israel was to be anointed. Had he told anyone his business for sacrificing and his preparation for anointing, it could have resulted in jealously among those in attendance as well as contempt from King Saul. Saul, who sat on the

## Chapter Two

throne of Israel, had rebelled against God, and God was calling Samuel to anoint a new king, a man after His own heart.

Jesse invited Prophet Samuel to his dwellings where his seven sons were waiting. "What a handsome family." Prophet Samuel thought. His eyes immediately fell upon Eliab, the eldest. He was tall, impressive, and charismatic and was a man of battle who fought with King Saul and his army against the Philistines. "Surely the Lord's anointed is before me." thought Samuel. He, however, heard a still small voice tell him, "Do not look at his appearance or the height of his stature, because I have rejected him; for God sees not as man sees, for man looks at the outward appearance, but the Lord looks at the heart." All of Jesse's sons, one by one, passed before Samuel. Samuel bypassed each brother saying, "Neither has the Lord chosen this one. That's not the man. No, not that one either. The Lord has not chosen these. Are these all the children?" Jesse said, "There remains yet the youngest of all and he is attending sheep in the fields. He is but a boy." Jesse had forgotten about his youngest son.

David wondered what could be so urgent that a lowly shepherd boy must leave his father's flocks with a keeper and quickly go home. Before entering Jesse's house, he removed his sandals and left them outside the front door, along with his rod and staff. As he entered his father's dwelling, it seemed all eyes were on him. His father, seven brothers, as

## In Spite of it All

well as a bent-over old man, had been standing waiting for him. Jesse said, "This is Prophet Samuel." He had heard of Prophet Samuel but had never met him. And there he stood right in front of him in his father's house! David noticed his long hair was wrapped in the shape of a crown on his head. Samuel's mother, Hannah, the wife of Elkanah, had dedicated him to God before he was even conceived, becoming a Nazarite. Nazarites were forbidden to cut their hair.

As a young boy, Samuel often heard the account from his mother how she poured out her soul before the Lord, because the Lord had closed her womb, and she had no children. She explained to Samuel, that year after year she would go up from her house in Ramah to the house of the Lord in Shiloh and pray for God to bless her with a baby. During one of those prayer times, she was weeping bitterly and greatly distressed. Through her tears, she made a vow and said, "O Lord of hosts, if Thou wilt indeed look on the affliction of Thy maidservant and remember me, and not forget Thy maidservant, but will give Thy maidservant a son, then I will give him to the Lord all the days of his life, and a razor shall never come on his head." Eli the priest had accused her of being drunk that day because only her lips were moving, but her voice was not heard. Hannah said, "Oh, no. I am a woman oppressed in spirit; I have drunk neither wine nor strong drink, but I have poured out my soul before the Lord."

## Chapter Two

Eli blessed her that day saying, "Go in peace; may the God of Israel grant your petition that you have asked of Him."

Hannah often told Samuel how God answered her desperate prayer and remembered her. "The Lord gave you to me," Hannah told Samuel. Samuel was only three years old when his mother weaned him and took him to live in the Temple and serve under Eli the priest. His mother told him how difficult it was for her to give him to Eli that day at Shiloh. She told Samuel she had made a promise to the Lord that if He blessed her with a son, she would dedicate him to the Lord all his life.

With tears running down her face and her heart heavy, Hannah carried the boy in her arms as she brought him to the Temple. She told Eli the priest, "Oh, my lord, I am the woman who stood here beside you praying to the Lord. For this child I prayed, and the Lord has given me my petition, which I asked of Him. So I have also dedicated him to the Lord; as long as he lives he is dedicated to the Lord." And Samuel worshiped the Lord there.

Samuel remembered the first time as a boy he heard God's voice. He was lying down in the Temple of the Lord where the ark was and heard his name called. He thought perhaps it was Eli calling for him, but Eli assured him it was not. A second time Samuel heard, "Samuel!" And Eli assured him again that he had not called him. And a third time Samuel

## In Spite of it All

heard a voice, and Eli once again assured him it was not he who called; but he instructed the young boy if he again heard his name called to respond with, "Speak, Lord, for Thy servant is listening." And a fourth time yet that night, the Lord came and stood and called as at other times, "Samuel! Samuel!" And Samuel responded as Eli had instructed him, "Speak for Thy servant is listening." God revealed to the young boy Samuel what He was about to do in Israel and thus anointed him as God's Prophet in Israel. Samuel grew and the Lord was with him and let none of his words fail.

Samuel remembered seeing both his father and mother once a year when they came to Shiloh to offer sacrifice and worship the Lord. He looked forward to them coming as Hannah would bring him a little linen ephod robe, she had made that year. He remembers one year seeing a baby in Hannah's arms. She told him Eli blessed her and God gave her another baby. It seemed like every year for the next several years, Hannah would have yet another baby in her arms, and toddlers and young children were running everywhere. Elkanah's family was growing! Every year Samuel looked forward to seeing and playing with his three brothers and two sisters. Samuel was growing in stature and favor both with the Lord and with men.

Prophet Samuel's loosely fitted mantle, made of sheepskin, had a V-neck opening at the neck, and slits in the two

## Chapter Two

corners for his arms. It was crudely sewed together, soiled, and well worn with holes throughout the garment. His mantle was a visible indication of his authority and responsibility as God's chosen spokesman showing he was wrapped in God's authority. His hands were dry and cracked from the weather. As an old man, his unkempt shabby beard covered many deep wrinkles in his face. Yet, his eyes sparkled, as he stood bent over. David saw confidence in an old man that expressed spiritual authority as David had never witnessed before. He was holy unto the Lord. He heard his oldest brother, Eliab, mumble, "You're supposed to be watching Father's sheep." He was always critical of his youngest brother. As the oldest, he was bitter Samuel had not anointed him. The look on Eliab's face showed he was disgusted with the smell of sheep that accompanied David when he walked in.

*Samuel heard an internal word from God telling him to anoint David as the next king of Israel.*

Prophet Samuel took his horn of olive oil and anointed David in the presence of his father and brothers. The oil ran down his head, over his tear-filled eyes, down his face, and onto his shepherd's tunic, soiled from working in the fields. Oil represented the presence of God. Prophet Samuel whispered in his ear, "You will be the next king." David felt God was with him.

## In Spite of it All

Samuel then left the house and went to his home city of Ramah, the center of his prophetic activity, which was eleven miles north of Bethlehem. He left Jesse and his eight sons standing in the house amazed at what had just transpired. Nobody said a word. Nobody except David knew what Prophet Samuel whispered in his ear. David left the house, put on his sandals, grabbed his rod and staff, and went back to Jesse's sheep on the Judean hillsides near Bethlehem to relieve the sheep keeper who had been watching the sheep while he went home.

When he went back to the field that day to tend Jesse's sheep, he felt different. He felt peaceful; yet, confident. Nothing had changed, externally, as far as he could tell. King Saul was still on the throne. He was still a shepherd boy.

He spent many months in solitude and obscurity tending Jesse's sheep. Sometimes it became monotonous. He became a marksman with his sling and stones, killing wild animals that neared his father's sheep. His sling was made from a small pouch of leather that was two feet long that could securely hold a stone. The sling worked best if the stones were smooth and about one and one-half inches in diameter. Smooth round stones would travel in a straight line. He placed the stone in the pouch and whirled the sling so that the stone was held in place by centrifugal force. When one of

## Chapter Two

the strings of leather was released, the stone would leave the pouch with tremendous force and intense speed.

He wrote and sang songs while playing his lyre to the sheep and the Lord. However, his songs seemed to come together with deeper meaning and greater satisfaction for his Heavenly Father since that day many months ago when Prophet Samuel came to his father's house. He drew from the inner strength of God's guidance.

*The Lord is my shepherd I shall not want. He makes me to lie down in green pastures. He leads me beside the still waters. He restores my soul. He leads me in the paths of righteousness for His Name's sake. Even though I walk through the valley of the shadow of death, I fear no evil; for Thou art with me. Thy rod and thy staff they comfort me. Thou prepares a table before me in the presence of my enemies. Thou has anointed my head with oil. My cup overflows. Surely goodness and mercy will follow me all the days of my life, and I will dwell in the house of the Lord forever.*

David was developing a reputation as a skillful musician, a mighty man of valor, a warrior, and one showing good judgment in conduct and speech. The Lord was with him.

King Saul had been disobedient to the Lord's direction. The Spirit of the Lord departed King Saul and God replaced the void with a manic, miserable paranoia disorder that kept him up at night and terrorized him during the day. He had

## In Spite of it All

learned of David's melodious music and sent messengers to Jesse to ask his permission to have David attend the king. David found favor in Saul's sight, as he was refreshed and calmed when David played. He made David his armor-bearer. David also continued to attend Jesse's sheep, killing both a lion and a bear when they took a lamb from the flock.

David remembered the confidence, courage, and strength he gained from God, as he went up against Goliath of Gath of the Philistines. King Saul, the men of Israel, and his three oldest brothers, Eliab, Abinadab, and Shammah went up against the Philistines in the valley of Elah morning and evening for forty days and; yet, no one was willing to accept the challenge of the nine-foot giant.

Jesse asked David to leave his sheep in the care of another shepherd, and take food to his brothers to the circle of camp where the Philistines and Israelites were preparing for battle. As he approached the valley of Elah, he left his baggage in the care of a baggage keeper and ran to the battle line and entered, in order to greet his brothers. As he was talking to them, the giant Goliath came up from the army of the Philistines. David had never heard of Goliath and inquired about the situation at hand asking what would be done for the man that kills the giant. The men of Israel said Saul would enrich the man who killed Goliath, give him his daughter in marriage, and make his father's house tax-free. David asked,

## Chapter Two

"Who is this uncircumcised Philistine, that he should taunt the armies of the living God?" His brother Eliab's anger burned against David and said, "Why have you come down? And with whom have you left those few sheep in the wilderness? I know the wickedness of your heart. You have come down to see the battle." David said, "For what have I done now? Was it just not a question?"

Saul sent for the boy, David, and asked about the words he spoke. David told Saul how God delivered him from the paw of both a lion and bear and asked if he could go up against the giant. Saul had David put on his garments and armor, but it was cumbersome and unfamiliar to him, and he took it off. David took his stick in his hand and carefully chose for himself five smooth stones from the Brook of Elah, and put them in his shepherd's bag, which he had. His sling was in his hand as he approached the giant. In the name of the Lord of Hosts, David ran quickly toward the battle line to meet the Philistine. He drew from his bag one of the five smooth stones, placed it in his sling, and slung it at the giant, sinking the stone deep into his forehead. Goliath fell on his face to the ground. As David ran and stood over the Philistine, he took Goliath's sword and killed him, cutting off his head with it. When David returned from killing Goliath with his head in his hand, Abner the commander of the army, brought him to Saul. Saul asked him whose son he was? David answered, "I

## In Spite of it All

am the son of your servant Jesse the Bethlehemite." He did not recognize him as the shepherd boy who used his gift of music to skillfully play for him in his courts to soothe his terrorized soul.

David was gaining popularity and prospering greatly in all his ways, for the Lord was with him. He became a national hero and people began to sing praises about him. Saul made David commander over his armies; he became a permanent part of his court, and gave him his daughter, Michal, in marriage. However, Saul developed jealously toward David because of the attention he was gaining. David fled from Saul for his life, leaving his wife Michal in Gibeah, and escaped to Ramah to Prophet Samuel where he found him supervising a community of prophets in the dwellings at Naioth.

David had long conversations with Samuel in Naioth. He told him all that Saul had done to him.

David wrote songs while he rested at Naioth.

*In the Lord I take refuge; How can you say to my soul, flee as a bird to your mountain; for, behold, the wicked bend the bow. They make ready their arrow upon the string. To shoot in darkness at the upright in heart. If the foundations are destroyed, what can the righteous do? The Lord is in His holy temple; the Lord's throne is in heaven; his eyes behold, his eyelids test the souls of men. The Lord tests the righteous and the wicked. And the one who loves violence His soul hates. Upon*

## Chapter Two

*the wicked He will rain snares; fire and brimstone and burning wind will be the potion of their cup. For the Lord is righteous; he loves righteousness; the upright will behold His face.*

David became a fugitive in the Judean wilderness, always on the run from Saul. He had attracted and formed a band of 600 followers in the Judean hills. These men became his private army, later the basis for a regular standing army, with thirty of them becoming an inner core of officers, hiding out in caves and taking refuge in the strongholds of Engedi. The cave of Engedi was an oasis in the wilderness with fresh-water springs and lush vegetation high above the Dead Sea. During an encounter with King Saul at Engedi when David had an opportunity to kill Saul, he chose not to. David said to his men, "Far be it from me, because of the Lord, that I should do this thing to my lord, the Lord's anointed, to stretch out my hand against him since he is the Lord's anointed." The Lord was with David.

Then Samuel died, and all Israel gathered together and mourned for him, and buried him at his house in Ramah. A holy man of God that was instrumental in David's young life was gone. David dared not go to his funeral as he was on the run from Saul. How he missed him. How he longed for conversation. Who would he go to with his questions about his anointing? "I'm a fugitive on the run from a mentally unstable king. How does this work?" "Oh, Samuel," David said out

## In Spite of it All

loud, wishing he could hear him. *"I am scared. I don't know how to be a king. I only know how to be a shepherd."*

David stayed on the run from Saul for many years. Saul and three of his sons, Jonathan, Abinadab, and Malchishua died with him in battle at Mount Gilboa. David deeply mourned the loss of his good friend and brother-in-law, Jonathan.

After the death of Saul, David traveled to the city of Hebron. While living there he acquired six wives, and six sons were born to him. David's house was strengthened. Then all the elders of the tribes of Israel came to David at Hebron and said, "Behold, we are your bone and your flesh. And the Lord said to you, 'You will shepherd my people Israel and you will be a ruler over Israel.'" They made a covenant with him before the Lord and anointed him king of Judea. David was thirty years old. He reigned over Judah at Hebron for seven and a half years. David moved his clan and his capital from Hebron to Jerusalem. He married more concubines and wives, and they had more sons and daughters. He was anointed king at Jerusalem over all the United Kingdom and ruled thirty-three years.

David was a godly man of prayer. As a shepherd boy, battlefield commander, and later king of Israel, he was reliable, hardworking, and intelligent. His artistic and creative attributes are seen in his sacred poetry. He wrote beautiful verses both in the good and bad times. He was respectful to

## Chapter Two

those in authority over him, a faithful soldier on the battlefield, well off financially, and blessed with good health, good looks, and steadfast faith in his God. He was considered the godly leader of the nation of Israel. God had placed His hand of blessing on David.

But, David sinned. His sin was very uncharacteristic of his lifestyle. It was costly to his spiritual, personal, family, and professional life. It was also a sin that dramatically impacted the life of a young Jewish woman named Bathsheba.

# CHAPTER THREE

Bathsheba was born into one of the most prominent families in Israel. Her grandfather, Ahithophel, was King David's personal advisor. Her father, Eliam, was also in David's army and selected by David as one of his thirty mightiest men.

Her birth name was Bathshua, which meant "Daughter of my Prosperity." Eliam's own prominent and prosperous position in David's kingdom was reflected in his daughter's name. His values later changed and he renamed her Bathsheba at her Bat-Mitzvah at the age of twelve and honored her by calling her "The Daughter of Oath," in relationship to the law.

She heard a knock on the door shortly before retiring for the evening. Her heart must have skipped a beat as she wondered who that could be at this hour. She went to the door and opened it. There stood two of King David's messenger soldiers. It took her breath away. One said, "Lady Bathsheba, you are being summoned by King David to the palace."

## In Spite of it All

Her mind raced a million miles an hour. To the palace? Did something happen to Uriah? Was her father in harm's way? What about her grandfather? She did not know the king was even in the city. She assumed that he had led the Israeli army into battle when Eliam and Uriah left last month. Whatever the reason for her being summoned by the king, she did not want to keep him waiting. She told them she needed to change clothes. She closed the door and left them standing outside. Her hands and legs trembled as she quickly walked to the back room. She took off her nightclothes and exchanged them for a blue tunic, and tucked her still damp hair under her headscarf.

She had just finished her monthly ritual purification mikveh. The Law of Moses instructed devout Jewish women to immerse themselves in a mikveh, at sunset, seven days after her monthly show of blood stopped. For most women, the ritual mikveh coincides fairly closely with the time of ovulation in the monthly cycle when a woman is most likely to conceive. Mikveh purification was also practiced before a woman's wedding, after childbirth, and by both husband and wife after sexual relations.

The body of water used for the mikveh was water caught from rain or spring water and water that had not been stored in a vessel. A mikveh could not be taken in a tub or stagnant pool of water and had to be flowing through the mikveh

## Chapter Three

pool. Uriah had built a mikveh on their home's patio courtyard. Mikvehs are a place of modesty used for ceremonial cleansing and purification. It was not a bathtub that could be moved. It was built to specific Jewish requirements. The law required the woman to be completely naked and completely immersed.

Bathsheba was not pregnant with Uriah's baby as evident by her observing her mikveh.

She grabbed her woolen cloak, put it over her tunic and clasped it closed, tied a sash around her middle, and slipped into her sandals that were sitting by the door. She checked the two oil lamps, which were burning. She wanted to be sure they were adequately filled, as she did not know how long she would be gone and did not want them to go out. She opened the door and saw the two soldiers standing where she left them. She closed the door behind her and the soldiers escorted her the short distance up the hill to the palace, entering through the servant's side entrance. A few minutes later they presented her to King David.

Bathsheba walked into the king's private bedroom, expecting to hear terrible news from the battlefield. But the king assured her that her father and husband had reported success from the front and she could be confident of their safety. He invited her to join him in dinner and wine. After some time, his intentions became evident and refusing the

## In Spite of it All

advances of her king seemed impossible for a woman whose family had spent their lives serving the monarch of their nation. Shocked and speechless, she found herself violated sexually by the spiritual leader she had respected since a child.

After he lay with her, she asked to purify herself from her uncleanness which she did in the palace mikveh, after which she returned to her house. She was in her own bed before the first break of light in the eastern sky. The king did not immerse in a mikveh after relations with Bathsheba.

Back in her bed, Bathsheba was unable to sleep, replaying over and over the events of the night. She felt embarrassed, violated, ashamed, and confused. She cried uncontrollably as her body shook until she was completely physically and emotionally exhausted.

She finally rose early the next morning, as was her routine. She changed from her bedclothes back into her blue tunic. She had no appetite for her normal breakfast of bread and olives. She put her head covering on, slipped on her sandals, picked up her large earthenware pitcher, placed it on her right shoulder, and walked to the local well to draw water for the day. While at the well, she ignored the normal chatter of the other women who had come to draw water. She wondered if they knew she had been at the palace with David the night before. No. Not possible. She was undercover by David's soldiers the entire night. They took an oath of silence.

## Chapter Three

It was between David and her. No one would ever know. She placed the pitcher, now heavy with water, on her right hip and walked home. Mid-morning Bathsheba walked to the local market to purchase the day's provisions, and then back home again. She put her provisions from the market away and swept the dirt floor.

She went out to the patio and stood by the mikveh, and relived in her mind, once more, the night's events. She stood staring up the hill to the palace and tears filled her eyes. David had observed her from his balcony while she was engaging in her ritual purification. She had no idea he was watching. How many other times, she wondered, had he stood on his balcony and watched her? Was he looking down on her now? She thought about his actions last night in his bedroom chambers. What was she to do when he advanced to her? He was the king and she was to obey his commands. She had no choice in the matter.

Her mother stopped over late morning and together they milled grain. Did her mother know about the events of last night? No, she did not. That was not possible. Later in the day, her mother went home, and she sat down at her loom to continue weaving her baby's blanket. She ate, alone in silence, her evening meal of bread, fruit, and figs, followed by a mug of water. It was growing dark. She lit the wicks in the oil lamps and went to bed.

## In Spite of it All

Her days were long. She and Uriah had been married for over a year and still they had not been blessed with a baby. Bathsheba's arms ached to hold the child she wanted so desperately to have. After their wedding celebration, she believed she would become pregnant on her wedding night. When Uriah marched off to battle against the Amalekites a month ago, she did not know how long he would be fighting before she saw him again. She missed him and wondered how she could ever explain what had happened at the palace.

To fight was a religious duty. Soldiers on active duty were required to remain in a sanctified state and deny themselves sexual relations while serving. When an Orthodox Jew when off to war, he would grant his wife a provisional divorce in case he was to die without leaving a corpse or without a witness. This would grant the wife the ability to divorce her husband in his absence.

Her show of blood did not come that month. Nor the next. Bathsheba did not want to believe what was happening to her body. Yet, she watched as her belly started to swell. It really could not be, could it; she was pregnant with the king's child? Really? How would she tell her father and mother? She was concerned about how her grandfather would receive the news of a baby born out of an adulterous relationship.

Bathsheba knew the act of adultery, according to the Law of Moses, was punishable by death by both parties involved.

## Chapter Three

Both she and David were going to die by being stoned to death. The thought was unimaginable and unfathomable. She was scared for her life as well as that of her unborn baby. She had never seen a stoning, but her father had told her about one he witnessed. It made her sick to her stomach. She felt alone and isolated. Whatever happened to David, anyway? After that night at the palace, she never saw or heard from him. She cried herself to sleep.

For weeks, her emotions were all over the place. She was in denial. She did not want to be pregnant in this way, with David's baby. It was not supposed to be like this. She wanted Uriah's baby. Maybe she would miscarry the baby. She thought about getting an abortion. She knew sometimes prostitutes needed this service, and she could contact one to find out how to kill her baby. Maybe she should sign the provisional divorce Uriah had drawn up, and become a beggar with a baby in the streets of Jerusalem. The king would never know about his baby.

Her emotions turned to anger. She was angry toward David for having her taken in the middle of the night and violating her. Anger because all he wanted was to satisfy his sexual fantasy and lust, using her for his pleasure. He knew Uriah was out of town. She was angry toward Uriah for not *getting* her pregnant by now. She became angry with God because she *was* pregnant. She was angry with herself for not

## In Spite of it All

refusing to go with the soldiers to the palace, or resisting the king's advances on that night two months ago, even though as a woman she was powerless.

Bathsheba started bargaining with God. "God of Abraham, Isaac, and Jacob, if you let something happen to this baby and it is not born, I promise to do charity work in the streets of Jerusalem the rest of my life."

She became depressed. For days she simply could not get out of bed without forcing herself to get up. She did not want life to be like this. She had faithfully served the God of Abraham, Isaac, and Jacob all her life. She tried hard to keep the Law of Moses. So why now? Why this? She felt there was no way out of her situation. It seemed her depression was so heavy some days she could hardly breathe.

She finally came to accept the reality of her situation. She was pregnant with King David's child. She could do nothing about it. If David, her baby, and she died according to the Jewish law, it was because they had broken the Law of Moses and it was required of those guilty of adultery.

She sent and told David, and said, "I am pregnant."

# CHAPTER FOUR

David received the note from his messenger and read it in private. It was not signed; yet, he knew it came from Bathsheba. He very carefully destroyed the message. David did not respond to its contents. However, immediately, in his mind, he started putting a plan together. He called for a messenger to deliver a message to Joab, who was still fighting on his behalf with the Israeli army. Joab was to inform Uriah that he was to leave the battlefield, come back to Jerusalem, and speak with the king.

Uriah ran all the way back to Jerusalem. He wondered if something had happened to Bathsheba and needed his attention. As he ran through the city gates attired in his battle armor, he noticed the elders sitting at the gates to the city. He ran past them and up to the palace. He was met by two security soldiers, who were expecting him, and ushered him into the palace, to David's quarters.

David answered the knock on his door, "Who is it?" One of the soldiers said, "Your security soldier, my lord." David

## In Spite of it All

opened the door and there stood Uriah, between the two soldiers. One said, "King David, we present you Commander Uriah." "Thank you," said David. "That is all." David led him through his bedroom chambers and onto his patio roof. It was late afternoon. They both stood for a moment looking toward Uriah's house. "Have a seat, Uriah," said David. "How is the welfare of Joab?" asked David. "War is never easy, my lord. The innocent fall in harm's way. That is difficult for me to see. Joab is an excellent commanding officer, and I do believe he works quite hard to serve you and the Israeli army. The brothers in the field are working together to defeat the Amalekites." Uriah continued, "The sun is hot on the battlefield, but we have an adequate water supply, and we are able to rest at day's end and enjoy an evening meal together." David said, "You are a proven soldier, Uriah."

There was additional dialog about war strategy for the next hour. "Evening is drawing nigh, Uriah, and you have been away from Bathsheba for several months. Go down to your house, enjoy your night, and have relations with her," said David. Uriah did not comment. He bowed to the king and went out of the king's presence. But Uriah slept at the door of the king's house with all the servants of his lord and did not go down to his house.

In the morning when Bathsheba went to the well to draw water, there was gossip among the women at the well that

## Chapter Four

Uriah was in the city and had met with King David last night. Someone asked Bathsheba if Uriah came to her? This was the first Bathsheba had heard of Uriah's return to Jerusalem. She assured them she did not know what they were talking about and the last time she saw Uriah was over three months ago when he went to war. As Bathsheba walked back to her house with her jug filled with water resting on her right hip, she felt a twinge somewhere in her belly. Was that David's baby moving? There it was again.

When she arrived back at her house, she set the jug of water on the table and sat down on a chair. She was feeling particularly pregnant this morning. Was Uriah really in Jerusalem meeting with David last night? Did David tell him of the baby? Would Uriah come home for a few hours? She was not even sure she wanted to see him. He would surely notice her enlarged belly under the bed covers. How would she explain her pregnancy?

Now when they told David, "Uriah did not go down to his house." David called for him and said to Uriah, "Have you not come from a journey? Why did you not go down to your house?" And Uriah said to David, "The ark and Israel and Judah are staying in temporary shelters, and my lord Joab and the servants of my lord are camping in the open field. Shall I then go to my house to eat and to drink and to lie with my wife? By your life and the life of your soul, I will not

## In Spite of it All

do this thing." Uriah also remembered the vow he took of celibacy while on active duty. Uriah was a better and more faithful soldier than David.

David ordered Uriah to spend the day at the palace in Jerusalem, and join him for the evening meal. The king provided quarters in the palace for him to rest, and have food delivered. As Uriah spent the day resting, his mind drifted to Bathsheba. He wondered how she was doing. He knew he could be gone to war as much as a year. That was a long time. How she so wanted to be pregnant with his baby before he left for war three months ago. He wondered if her days were long. He caught a glimpse of their house from David's patio roof when he and David were having the evening meal together. He wondered if he might see Bathsheba in the courtyard. David ordered several flasks of wine as they sat on his patio roof talking about war and life.

Toward midnight, after David got Uriah drunk with wine, for the second time in twenty-four hours, he told Uriah to go down to his wife and have relations with her. Uriah still had enough sense about him to know he did not want to break his vow of celibacy, and again slept on the palace steps with the king's servants.

In the morning when David learned Uriah had again slept at the palace, he was angry. Seeing his plan to cover his adultery had failed, he wrote a letter to Joab saying, "Place Uriah

## Chapter Four

in the front line of the fiercest battle and withdraw from him, so that he might be struck down and die." David handed the message to Uriah, sealed with wax with his signature ring, and told him to deliver it to Joab.

David had arranged for Uriah to be murdered. Uriah carried his own death sentence back to the front!

Uriah left the king's palace and ran past the elders in the city who were still sitting discussing the Law of Moses, back through the city gates, and on to the Israeli camp. "A message for you, my lord, from the king," said Uriah. He handed the sealed message to Joab, who took the note back to his tent and read it in private. He reread the message two more times. He wondered to himself if the king had gone mad. Had he lost his sense of obligation and responsibility to his soldiers who were fighting on his behalf? Uriah was one of his thirty mightiest soldiers.

Joab remembered when Saul had gone mad, and for a decade, David was a fugitive on the run from him in the Judean wilderness. That was when Joab joined him and his six hundred followers to place a ring of protection around David. Many of those men became the Israeli army and were still fighting on David's behalf. David was the King but also family. He is my uncle. Joab was torn between questioning David's authority and following his orders. He reasoned

## In Spite of it All

with himself and knew it was not his place, however, to ask questions.

Joab strategized his battle plans to besiege the city of Rabbah to ensure Uriah would be killed in battle. The men of the city went out and fought against Joab, and some of the people among David's servants fell, and Uriah the Hittite also died. Uriah's death seemed to the Israelites just another war casualty.

Joab sent and reported to David all the events of the war. And he charged the messenger that when he finished telling all the events of the war to the king, that if it happens he becomes angry and wonders why they went so close to the wall to fight, then you shall say, "Your servant Uriah the Hittite is dead also."

David told the messenger, "Thus, you shall say to Joab, 'Do not let this thing displease you, for the sword devours one as well as another; make your battle against the city stronger and overthrow it;' and so encourage him."

# CHAPTER FIVE

Bathsheba answered the knock on her door. It was early afternoon. As she opened the door, two soldiers stood there. For a few moments she had a flashback to the night she was taken to the palace. "Lady Bathsheba, the secretary of the Israeli Army regrets to inform you that your husband, Uriah the Hittite, was killed by archers in battle this morning as he and his infantry were besieging the city of Rabbah. His corpse has been brought by stretcher back to Jerusalem and it is ready to be prepared for burial. It is outside the city walls guarded by four soldiers." Bathsheba immediately tore her tunic, as this was the Jewish practice of mourning. They left as quickly as they arrived and Bathsheba closed the door.

Bathsheba grabbed her belly. David's baby. She felt weak in the knees. She had to sit down. Right on the floor. Right where she was. It felt like she couldn't breathe. Maybe she misunderstood the soldier. How could he be dead? She became overwhelmed with tears when she saw Eliam and her mother walk in the door. The town gossip spread quickly of

## In Spite of it All

Uriah's death and she could hear wailing and lamentation announcing to the neighborhood that a death had taken place. They held each other and sobbed. "Father, is Uriah really dead?" Bathsheba asked. "Yes, my daughter, he is dead. We must go to his body now and prepare it for his burial as it is hot outside, and his body can rapidly decompose."

The three of them walked arm in arm through the city streets and out the gates of Jerusalem. Wailers started following them. They approached Uriah's body and Bathsheba bent down on her knees to lift the cloth that laid gently over him. She sobbed as she looked at his wounds from the arrows that killed him. Blood had dried on his body and a stench was starting to rise.

He was such a handsome and faithful man of God and faithful to David in all respects. Eliam and some other men moved the body from the stretcher to the ground. Someone brought her water to wash his body. It was not pleasant, but it was an honor to prepare her husband for his burial. It was a holy moment. She securely closed his eyes and mouth with a linen wrap someone handed her and tied it around his chin. She trimmed his nails and hair and anointed him with oils and ointment that someone else gave her. She looked up and there was her brother Machir and Mephibosheth. She wanted to hug both of them, but she was unclean, as she had touched Uriah's corpse. The Law of Moses forbids such a

## Chapter Five

practice until she had become ritually clean by washing after preparing his body. She thanked them for coming. She left his military attire on and gently wrapped his body in a linen cloth. Eliam, Machir, and the two soldiers who came to her door that morning announcing his death placed his body on a bier. Bathsheba placed his shield under his head and his sword on his right side. They carried him to the burial cave, outside the city, that Eliam had purchased for the family several years ago. A large stone was placed in front of the tomb to seal it.

David observed the activities of Uriah's burial procession from his palace.

It was over. It happened so quickly. It was nearly dark now. Bathsheba could hear the wailers throughout the streets as she and her mother and father walked back to her house. "Father," Bathsheba said. "What do I do now?" Eliam replied, "We grieve for Uriah for thirty days, as is the custom of our culture. I think it will happen quite naturally, my daughter."

Bathsheba put on a black tunic and covered her head. She did no household or community chores, including personal hygiene for seven days. The ladies she met at the well in the mornings brought in food for several days. On the seventh day, Bathsheba went outside for the first time. Her mother escorted her to Uriah's gravesite. She spent several minutes pondering the week's activities. As she stood at the gravesite,

## In Spite of it All

she felt David's baby becoming more active in her belly. She had never told her mother of the pregnancy. She did not know how or when she would. She didn't know what her future held. She was widowed at the age of sixteen. Eliam said she could come back and live with him and her mother.

At the end of thirty days of grieving for Uriah, Bathsheba took off her black mourning attire and replaced it with her blue tunic. She surmised she was four months pregnant with David's baby. She heard a knock at the door the morning of the thirty-first day after Uriah's death. She was surprised when, once again, two soldiers stood at her door and said, "King David is summoning you to the palace." She was emotionally and physically tired and apprehensive. The soldiers took her to the palace and, once again, presented her to King David. Bathsheba was uncomfortable returning to the palace.

"Bathsheba, I want to marry you. You have no one to care for you since Uriah's death. You can join my harem," said David. "His harem?" thought Bathsheba. "Is that all he thinks of me is another wife to add to his collection?" The king continued, "We will have the baby and all of Israel will believe it was conceived on our wedding night, tonight."

With little to no social standing as a young widow in the Jewish nation, Bathsheba was virtually forced into marriage. What other option was there for her? She was thrust

## Chapter Five

into a vast political bureaucracy and personal harem created by King David. She moved into the palace that night as the eighth wife of King David. They did not engage in sexual relations because of her pregnancy according to Jewish custom. David touched her growing belly, which bore his child. That was the full extent of his attempt to comfort and assure her he was doing what was best for both of them and the child she bore. The next day she and the two maidservants David had given her, went down to her house to collect items and she completed her move into quarters in the palace David had designated for her. It was strange; yesterday she was the widow of Uriah the Hittite, and today she was the eighth wife of the king of Israel, pregnant with his baby and living in the palace.

The kings of Israel were instructed not to multiply wives for themselves. David, however, chose to ignore this instruction set forth in the Mosaic Law and increased the number of his wives and concubines while he served as the king of Israel. Polygamy was accepted in that day among the kings of the Middle East and collecting a large harem added to the king's honor. Yet, polygamist marriage violated God's law.

For the next few months until the birth of their baby, David lived with emotional turmoil and anguish while attempting to cover his sins of the past. He continued to judge the nation of Israel, yet his heart was filled with guilt. God's

## In Spite of it All

hand of conviction was pressing hard on David's heart. He felt as if he were suffocating. But he chose to ignore God's hand in his life.

Shortly after their marriage, it was rumored Bathsheba was pregnant. David and Bathsheba did not deny this rumor, only affirmed it was true. On nights David called for Bathsheba to come to his chambers they briefly talked about the baby she was carrying. David felt his plan was going smoothly, except for the nagging he felt in his heart. He did not tell Bathsheba about Uriah's murder.

As one of David's wives, her maidservants now did the usual household activities she had grown used to doing every day. Her midwives were the best in all of Israel. Occasionally, her mother would come to the palace. It was on one of these visits while sitting in her chambers with her mother, she broke down and shared about the night David summoned her to his palace for his pleasure. They talked and cried into the late hours of the night. Bathsheba invited her mother to stay until morning.

There were so many wives, concubines, and children in the palace! She and David's third wife, Abigail, gravitated toward conversation. Abigail was intelligent and spiritual and Bathsheba gained wisdom from their conversations. She watched as the other wives and concubines tended to their children. It seemed chaotic to Bathsheba. She continued to

## Chapter Five

study the Law of Moses as she remembered it from her youth when her mother would instruct her at home. She became proficient at looking for wool and flax at the market and working with her hands. As a wife of the king, her clothing changed from her one blue tunic to fine linen and purple. She enjoyed bringing food from the market to give to the chefs to try new recipes.

Several months later, after the evening meal, she felt birth pangs. She had her maidservant call her midwives, as well as her mother. David was alerted that Bathsheba was in labor in her quarters. Bathsheba labored throughout the night. Early the next morning she gave birth to a son. He did not appear healthy at his birth, however, and was lethargic. Neither did he cry when he was born. Her midwives washed him, rubbed salt over his skin, bound him tightly, and swaddled him with five feet of bandages five inches wide. The baby had difficulty latching on to breast-feed and a wet nurse was called to the palace to nurse the boy. David was informed he had a son.

*But the thing that David had done was evil in the sight of the Lord.*

The afternoon of his son's birth, the Lord sent Prophet Nathan to David to bring him to his senses. David invited him into the palace. David knew and respected Nathan. As the king sat on his throne with his men of council in the room,

## In Spite of it All

Prophet Nathan stood in front of David and told a story of a rich man and a poor man. The rich man had everything. In spite of this, he stole the poor man's only lamb and roasted it for a traveler, who came as a guest to his house. This story made David angry and said the man deserved to die. The story compared David, the rich man, with Uriah, the poor man, and the ewe was Bathsheba. Nathan confronted David with, "You are the man!"

Prophet Nathan reprimanded David. Thus says the Lord God of Israel. "It is I who anointed you king over Israel and it is I who delivered you from the hand of Saul. I also have given you your master's house and your master's wives into your care. I gave you the house of Israel and Judah; and if that had been too little, I would have added to you many more things like these! Why have you despised the word of the Lord by doing evil in His sight? You had Uriah the Hittite struck down with the sword." Nathan explained to David the consequences of his sins of adultery, rape, and murder:

*The sword shall never depart from your house. Evil will rise up against you from your own house. Your wives will be given to your son and he will lie with them in broad daylight.*

David became overwhelmed with conviction, took off his crown and threw it on the floor, and fell on his knees sobbing before Prophet Nathan. Then David said to Nathan, "I have sinned against the Lord." He recognized the depths of his

## Chapter Five

sins and was repentant. He sobbed for a long period of time on his knees as everyone stood in the room silently watching him.

God spoke through Nathan and forgave him. Nathan said, "The Lord has taken away your sin; you shall not die." God granted mercy and forgiveness to David because of his genuine and immediate repentance and he would not be stoned to death.

Nathan now pronounced perhaps the severest consequence of his sins:

*The child that is born to you shall surely die.*

Nathan left the throne room and went home while David was still on his knees, sobbing.

The palace physicians were called to Bathsheba's bedside as she held the baby. They said there was nothing that could be done for the child. The midwives sent a message to David early that evening that his baby was very sick. David went to Bathsheba's quarters and greeted her. One of the midwives handed him his son to hold. He seemed so small and fragile. His breathing was labored as David watched his chest barely rise and fall under his swaddled clothes. Tears were running down David's cheeks. "My lady," said David, "Prophet Nathan was in the palace this afternoon. He told me, because of my sins, our son is going to die. I am going to inquire of God for the child and pray and fast." He handed his son back to

## In Spite of it All

the midwife and gently touched Bathsheba's cheek. She was crying.

He lay all night on the ground. And the elders of his household stood beside him to raise him up from the ground, but he was unwilling and would not eat food with them.

Bathsheba never came out of her quarters. She wanted as much uninterrupted time with her baby as possible. Abigail visited her the day after the birth of her son. Abigail said, "I had a son with David while we lived in Hebron and named him Chileab. Sometimes we called him Daniel. He was not well, either. He was slow of speech and seemed confused when I tried to talk to him. He, like your son, Bathsheba, did nothing wrong. He died at the age of seven. That was our only child. It was a very sad day for me when I buried my son. My heart was heavy with sadness, and yes, anger. I had to make the choice, though, to be angry the rest of my life, or help heal my brokenness by ministering to women in similar situations." Abigail continued, "I was in the palace the night David summoned you to his quarters. I was aware of the soldiers sneaking you in through the servant's side entrance. However, it was not my business or place to intercept the business of the king. I did pray for you that evening and heard you leave early the next morning." They hugged and Abigail left.

## Chapter Five

The baby gradually grew weaker, refused to eat, and slept most of the time. He died in Bathsheba's arms on his seventh day of life.

The servants of David were afraid to tell him that the child was dead, for they said, "Behold while the child was still alive, we spoke to him and he did not listen to our voice. How then can we tell him that the child is dead since he might do himself harm?" But when David saw that his servants were whispering together, David perceived that the child was dead; so David said to his servants, "Is the child dead?" And they said, "He is dead." David arose from the ground, washed, anointed himself, and changed his clothes; and he came into the house of the Lord and worshiped. He came to his own house and requested food set before him, and he ate.

His servants were confused by his behavior. They asked, "Why is it that when your son was alive you fasted and wept, but when the child died you arose and ate?" David said, "While the child was still alive, I fasted and wept; for I said 'who knows, the Lord may be gracious to me, that the child may live.' But now that he is dead, why should I fast? Can I bring him back again? I shall go to him, but he will not return to me."

In less than a year, Bathsheba attended the second funeral of a family member, her unnamed, uncircumcised

## In Spite of it All

seven-day-old baby. This time, however, David was by her side as she prepared the boy for his burial. Together they laid him on the floor of the king's throne room, right where David had lain prostrate for seven days. They carefully washed his body, closed his eyes and mouth with a linen wrap, and tied it around his small chin. They wrapped a small linen shroud around him and David carried him to his burial plot outside the gates of the city to a tomb purchased by the king for the royal family. Together they placed his body inside the tomb and had it secured with a large stone.

Both David and Bathsheba stayed in the palace the following week and wore black attire mourning the death of their baby. They refused visitors. They talked. It was something quite unusual for a couple to spend seven days alone, but David needed to confess the full extent of his sins to Bathsheba.

*"My lady, I am sorry for the pain I have caused you. I am responsible. I saw you from my patio roof and wanted you. As the king, I knew I could have anything I wanted, at any expense. My desire for you overwhelmed me and I violated you in an act of adulterous lust. You suffered by becoming pregnant with my child and did not make public the abuse of my power over you. I abused my power further. I ordered your husband Uriah to come home from the battlefield so he could sleep with you so that all of Israel would believe your child was*

## Chapter Five

*his son. He, however, was a better soldier than I and would not break his vow of celibacy. I became angry at his failure to fulfill my plan to cover my sin. So I sent him back into battle with sealed orders to his commanders, with the intent that he would become a casualty of war. His death was carried out by my orders."*

*When Prophet Nathan was here the afternoon of our baby's birth, he reprimanded me. As the result of my sin, the sword shall never depart my house; evil will rise from my own family, and my wives and concubines will be given to my companion and he will lie with them in broad daylight. The most severe punishment, Bathsheba, was the inevitable death of our child. I sincerely confessed my sins to God, and Prophet Nathan said I would not die but have to live with the consequences of my sins the rest of my life."*

*"Bathsheba, while I was praying and fasting for the seven days our son was sick, I asked God to be gracious to me according to His loving kindness. To blot out my transgressions. To wash me thoroughly from my iniquity, and cleanse me from my sin. I confessed my sin to God and God alone. I have sinned and done what is evil in God's sight. I asked him to purify me with hyssop, to become clean, and to wash me whiter than snow. I asked Him to allow me once more to experience joy and gladness.*

## In Spite of it All

*My lady, I remember how satisfied and peaceful I was walking with the Lord. I became arrogant and proud. I asked God to not cast me away from His presence, and not take His Holy Spirit from me, but to restore to me the joy of my salvation, and sustain me with a willing spirit. I had a broken spirit, a broken and contrite heart.*

*When I kept silent about my sin, my body wasted away through my groaning all day long. For day and night, God's hand was heavy upon me; my vitality was drained away as with the fever heat of summer. I acknowledged my sin to God, and my iniquity I have not hidden. I confessed my transgressions to the Lord, and He forgave the guilt of my sins."*

When David finished, they both held each other and cried. Bathsheba said, "My lord, I am not without sin. May God have mercy on us."

On the seventh day of their child's death, together they walked to his grave and stood before his tomb. Nothing was said. Nothing needed to be said. It was a holy moment.

According to the Law of Motherhood after giving birth to a son, the mother was unclean for forty days. At dusk on the fortieth day, Bathsheba purified herself by immersion in a mikveh. David went into Bathsheba and lay with her. She became pregnant. The pregnancy went well, and Abigail was happy for her. Bathsheba became quite good at making linen garments and selling them and supplying belts to the

## Chapter Five

tradesmen. She rose while it was still night and gave food to her ten maidservants. David had now given her eight more because of the responsibilities she was taking on in the palace. She rose up as a leader among the wives and concubines in the palace, and several of them would seek out her wisdom. She seemed to have endless energy and often invited one or more of the women and children in the palace to walk with her to take food to the needy in the streets. Bathsheba had a profound influence on the harem, as well as King David.

When it was time to deliver her baby, she sent for her midwives, two of her maidservants, and her mother. She delivered a son, without complications. Her midwives washed and rubbed him with salt, wrapped him in swaddling clothes, and handed him to Bathsheba. He latched on to breast-feed. Bathsheba was elated! A message was sent to David that Bathsheba had delivered a healthy son. He went to Bathsheba's quarters where the midwife handed his swaddled son to him to hold. He thanked God and Bathsheba for a healthy son.

On the eighth day of the baby's life, David and Bathsheba had a family celebration in the palace. Her father and mother, Machir her brother, Mephibosheth the crippled son of Jonathan who lived in the palace, Bathsheba's maidservants, Abigail and Prophet Nathan were at the celebration. Her grandfather Ahithophel did not come to the celebration.

## In Spite of it All

The priest Zadok came to the palace to perform the circumcision and blessing. When he asked what the child's name would be, David said "Solomon," which meant "peaceful."

# CHAPTER SIX

Bathsheba enjoyed watching her toddler, Lemuel, the family name she had given to Solomon, play in the palace gardens. Some of his half brothers by David's other wives and concubines were as much as twenty years older, and were out of the palace and fighting on behalf of the Israeli Army. The sons born to David and Bathsheba following Solomon's birth were named Nathan, Shobab, and Shammua. She invested in her sons' lives and encouraged them to gain understanding and sound teaching from the Law of Moses, to follow the instruction of their father, David, and to "Acquire wisdom! Acquire understanding!" She instructed them the fear of the Lord is the beginning of wisdom.

King David and Bathsheba explained to them the foolishness of their own sins of the past, and how they learned from their errors. They reminded their sons the God of Abraham, Isaac, and Jacob had forgiven them but that there was a price to be paid. Nathan's pronouncement of God's judgment for

## In Spite of it All

their sin was very specific. The death of their firstborn and family turmoil was the result of that sin.

Evil arose in the house of David. One of his sons, Amnon, was in love with his beautiful virgin half-sister, Tamar, and violated her. Now when King David heard of all these matters, he was very angry but he failed to discipline his son. The punishment for rape, according to the law, was death. David's older children resented this failure of their father to act and two years later Absalom, Tamar's brother, took matters into his own hands and killed Amnon.

Absalom fled Jerusalem but later returned. His relationship with David continued to deteriorate and he sought ways to overthrow David and become king of Israel. Over several years he attracted over two hundred key men, including Bathsheba's grandfather Ahithophel. While Bathsheba had forgiven the king, her grandfather, who was his closest advisor, could not.

One day, a messenger came to David, saying, "The hearts of the men of Israel are with Absalom." And David said to all his servants who were with him at Jerusalem, "Arise, and let us flee, for otherwise none of us shall escape from Absalom." The king and his entire household fled Jerusalem. He left ten concubines to keep the house. Someone told David, "Ahithophel is among the conspirators with Absalom." David prayed the counsel Ahithophel gave Absalom would be foolish.

## Chapter Six

David wrote a verse to calm his anxiety and keep his focus on the Lord.

*Lord, every day I have more enemies. Many people fight me. Many people say about me, "God will not save him." But Lord, you are a shield over me. You are my glory. You have lifted up my head. I shouted aloud to the Lord. He answered me from His holy mountain. I lay down and slept. I awoke because the Lord kept me alive. He kept me safe. I will not be afraid of 10,000 enemies that are all 'round me. Lord, stand up! My God, save me! In the past, you hit all my enemies in the face. You broke their teeth. It was the Lord that saved us. Lord, do good things for all your people.*

Now in all Israel, there was no one as handsome as Absalom, so highly praised; from the sole of his foot to the crown of his head, there was no defect in him. When he cut the hair of his head every year, because it was heavy, his hair weighed five pounds. Then Absalom and all his people, the men of Israel, entered Jerusalem, and Ahithophel with him. Then Absalom said to Ahithophel, "Give your advice. What shall we do?" Ahithophel said to Absalom, "Go into your father's concubines, whom he has left to keep the house; then all Israel will hear that you have made yourself odious to your father." So they pitched a tent for Absalom on the roof, and Absalom went in to his father's concubines in the sight of all of Israel, fulfilling another of the prophecies of Nathan.

## In Spite of it All

Ahithophel continued to advise Absalom, but he did not inquire of the Lord. He was wise in his own mind. The Lord had ordained to confuse the good counsel of Ahithophel, so the Lord might bring calamity on Absalom. When Ahithophel urged Absalom to pursue David, his counsel was rejected. As a result, he saddled his donkey and arose and went home, to his city, and set his house in order, and hanged himself; thus he died and was buried in the grave of his father.

Now Absalom happened to meet the servants of David as he was fighting the armies of Israel against his father. He was riding on his mule as the animal went under the thick branches of a great oak tree and his long locks became entangled in a tree branch and he was left hanging between heaven and earth until one of David's soldiers took three spears and thrust them through the heart of Absalom while he was yet alive in the midst of the oak. And ten more men gathered around and struck Absalom and killed him.

David grieved the losses in his life. Especially Absalom, whom he dearly loved. Is this what Prophet Nathan meant when he said David's house would never be at peace?

The king was restored to Jerusalem.

He continued to judge the nation of Israel until he was nearly seventy years old. He was not perfect, but he served a perfect God. Bathsheba had a profound influence on King David. From the point of his confession, his life dramatically

## Chapter Six

changed and his relationship with God became intimate in a way he had never known. His psalms were the most beautiful Bathsheba had ever heard as she listened to him sing and play his lyre.

*Blessed be the Lord God, the God of Israel, who alone works wonders. And blessed be His glorious name forever; and may the whole earth be filled with his glory. Amen, and Amen.*

He never took another wife or concubine after marrying Bathsheba. He did not fall into moral sin again throughout the balance of his life. Bathsheba gained the respect of her husband and became his favorite wife and close advisor.

Now David was old, advanced in age; and they covered him with clothes, but he could not keep warm. A young beautiful virgin, Abishag, was brought in to attend the king, nurse him, and lie with him. However, the king did not cohabit with her. While his father was dying, Adonijah, the king's oldest living son, after the deaths of Chileab, Amnon, and Absalom, exalted himself saying, "I will be king." He also was a very handsome man. He was making arrangements for his own coronation ceremony. However, he did not invite Prophet Nathan, Benaiah one of the mighty men, and Solomon his brother.

Bathsheba sat by the bedside of her king reflecting on their life together. She grew to love David, not only as her husband and king but also as the father of their five sons.

## In Spite of it All

She sometimes thought about their unnamed son that died at seven days, but the emotional pain had healed. She trained up her sons in the way of the Lord, trusting they would not depart from it. Solomon was now twenty years old. Her king was growing weaker each day but still recognized her, was clear of mind, and able to talk for brief periods of time.

Prophet Nathan informed Bathsheba about the plans of Adonijah to crown himself the new king before David had died or made known his desire to name Solomon the next king of Israel. The two of them informed the king of Adonijah's plans, prompting David to declare Solomon his successor to his throne.

Zadok the priest, Prophet Nathan, Benaiah of the mighty men, the Cherethites and the Pelethites, a group of elite mercenaries employed by King David, went down with Solomon as he rode King David's mule east of the city of David to the Kidron Valley, to the Spring of Gihon. There Zadok anointed Solomon with a horn of oil. As they rode back into Jerusalem, trumpets were blown, flutes played, and great rejoicing, so that the earth shook at their noise. And all the people, said, "Long live King Solomon." And King David was blessed that the God of Israel granted Solomon to sit on his throne for his own eyes to see.

As David's time to die drew near, he charged Solomon his son saying, *"Be strong and show yourself a man. And keep the*

## Chapter Six

*charge of the Lord your God, to walk in His ways, to keep His statutes, His commandments, His ordinances, and His testimonies according to what is written in the Law of Moses that you may succeed in all that you do and wherever you turn, so that the Lord may carry out His promise which He spoke concerning me, saying 'If your sons are careful of their way, to walk before Me in truth with all their heart and with all their soul, you shall not lack a man on the throne of Israel.'"*

Shortly after dawn the next day, David took his final breath. Bathsheba was his only wife by his side. It was a holy moment. She sobbed as she grieved for her lord. She and Solomon sat with his body for a few minutes before she released his corpse to the funeral bearers to prepare for burial. Wailing and lamentation could already be heard in the streets announcing King David had died. Bathsheba bowed for the last time to her king, told him good-bye, and walked out of his bedroom on the arm of her son, King Solomon.

Bathsheba and Solomon changed into black mourning attire. King David was buried that afternoon in his royal burial plot. One week after David's death, Solomon escorted his mother to David's grave. They stood quietly until Bathsheba said, "My king, Solomon, indeed David was a man after God's own heart."

After thirty days of mourning, Bathsheba and Solomon changed from their mourning clothes into brightly colored

## In Spite of it All

tunics. King Solomon had a throne made for Bathsheba and she sat on his right. She was the queen of all Israel!

King Solomon had a personal and tender heart for his mother as reflected in recorded proverbs from instructions his mother taught him as a child, as well as a young king. He recorded drunkenness leads to destruction, to judge fairly regardless of a person's financial well-being, and to defend the rights of the poor and needy. It is the responsibility of the king of Israel to be responsible and fair. He honored his mother by recording the attributes of a virtuous woman. He had observed Bathsheba's godly character as she lived in the palace married to David, and the parents of his three brothers and himself.

Bathsheba was a godly woman of dignity and grace. She was a Jewish woman who gained wisdom because she chose to trust God and honor her husband. She was wise, artistic, and an active homemaker tending to the needs of her servants and maids in the harem, serving them before the sun came up. At the same time, she was a businesswoman who made wise purchases, but not independently of her husband.

She was wealthy because she was the king's wife and it showed in the clothes she wore, yet she did not neglect the needs of the poor. While Bathsheba recognized beauty fades, the things of God and honoring him are desirable and lasting. Solomon and her other sons rose up and blessed her.

## Chapter Six

Bathsheba was a devout Jewish teenager married to a leading army commander, living at a time we recognize as the beginning of the most prosperous in the history of the nation of Israel. King David, a man she trusted and whom her family knew well, raped her. That same man murdered her husband, Uriah. Then the child she bore as a result of all of this died shortly after birth.

In spite of it all, adultery, rape, and murder, she was not destroyed emotionally by these events that invaded her life over a matter of months. Instead, she survived and had a dramatically positive influence on the king who had initiated all of these events, and even more so on the next king, Solomon. She ruled alongside this young king as the queen and continued to influence him as reflected in his words found in Proverbs 31. Her sons, while the youngest in King David's family, were never named among those who troubled him during his lifetime. In fact, in the genealogy of Christ, two of these sons are named. Solomon is in the linage of Joseph, the husband of Mary; and, Nathan in the linage of the Virgin Mary, mother of Jesus.

In spite of it all, God used Bathsheba, a woman of faith, in unparalleled ways, to bring about His plan for all mankind.

# ACKNOWLEDGMENTS

I would like to thank
- My husband Dennis for encouraging me to share the facts surrounding the scriptural account of Bathsheba,
- Sandy Wood for her review for biblical accuracy, and
- Elaine Penn for grammar and proofing of the manuscript.

www.ingramcontent.com/pod-product-compliance
Lightning Source LLC
Chambersburg PA
CBHW070102100426
42743CB00012B/2633